CAN
I DO?
THIS?

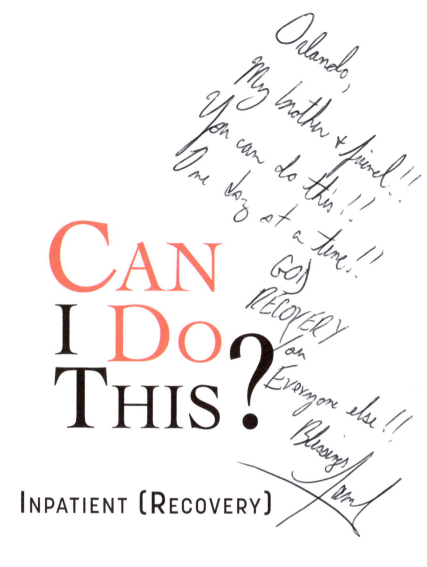

CAN I DO THIS ?

INPATIENT (RECOVERY)

JAMEL FREEMAN

XULON PRESS

Xulon Press
2301 Lucien Way #415
Maitland, FL 32751
407.339.4217
www.xulonpress.com

Paperback ISBN-13: 978-1-66285-618-1
Hard Cover ISBN-13: 978-1-66285-619-8
Ebook ISBN-13: 978-1-66285-620-4

TABLE OF CONTENTS

CHAPTER 1

THE BEGINNING TO "NEW"

I t is my initial day. There are so many thoughts. How did it come to this? I know, my stupid actions of driving drunk and not staying my ass at home. Now, I got to go into this rehab place, not know-ing anyone and having to communication with people I do not know. My first initial thought is, *leave me alone, l*et me get in my time and get the heck out of here. I am not even at this place yet, and I am having all these thoughts. What is it going to be like? Am I doing the right thing? I cannot talk to anyone, but I got GOD! I need to remember this. I am traveling with my girl and running errands before we reach our destination late this afternoon. The time is approaching and we are an hour out from our destination. One of the staff is calling me, asking about my whereabouts. I'm like, why this guy is so pressed? Anyhow, I am here. Let us get on with this.

Everyone is so welcoming. Smiles are everywhere. "Are they for real?" is the question I ask myself. Me, Hmmm, I will play this game, but honestly, how long can I play this? Being fake and keeping my mouth shut is not my thing. Oh, well, let us get this magical show on the road. The staff is striving to help me feel comfortable. I've got a headache, and my jaw hurts from this accident. I just want my meds and to be left alone but I've got to speak to ewwveryone. I am not really feeling this, and is this really going to work? Honestly, my thought was, no one in my family on either side has done this that I know of. I'm sure none of

1

my friends have. What if GOD is really giving me a new start? Meaning, I know challenges, test, and temptations will surface, but I can manage them better. Yes, I am admitting that I am an alcoholic. Never thought that these words would come out my mouth, but they just did. Till this day, accepting this name is a challenge for me. This is what made me like this and right now, this is who I am.

There is a change ahead. Let us see. I must do something. I am making this book simple but relatable. To those who struggled, wrestled, contemplated, and even left and came back, this is real. "Can I Do This?" The first, or half, of the day is over. I am done. Goodnight.

CHAPTER 2

ME

H ow can I start with myself? There are so many positive attributes with awfully bad decisions made, let alone an addiction to alcohol that I never thought I had. Figuring this out at the age of forty-two for me was like, "Wow." I am pointing at myself in the mirror and calculating all the negative experiences in my life with this terrible substance abuse. No, not Jamel. Yes, you, Jamel.

This all happened in a blink of any eye like it was yesterday. I will try to give you the full spectrum of this Friday, day and night. It was your typical weekend coming up, and I just got off work early Friday morning. I was exhausted, a little, but not a lot. My version of a good weekend was just relaxing with a couple of drinks, which I felt I earned, and just catching up on my responsibilities. The gym was a priority to me because I wanted to keep up on my youthful look but also keep up with my inspirational post on FB (Face-book) and IG (Instagram). Striving to remember back on this day is so vague yet also so real. This experience has been life-changing due to that night when I faced my near-death experience. As my day went on, I could not wait for that first drink, and not also remembering what led me to this point of drinking till I blacked out. Being a bachelor was not bad. Having the house to myself and drinking and feeling relaxed had my night going so smooth. Living in the city was so chill. I investigated the streets of downtown from the fourth-floor window of my apartment in the living room, and it was relaxing, therapeutic, as I may say. Going to the liquor store between what I call Jamel's sessions was the best and smoking a Black & Mild just increased the buzz feeling. Having contacted my cousin, or should I say responding to his text message, I thought going to see him was a good idea. I was not thinking about how much alcohol I had consumed, and it never crossed my mind if was even safe for me to drive. What a dumb ass I was, not thinking of my already bad decisions and a DUI charge still pending. In this case, I was acting like my father when I would see him drinking and just doing non-thinking things, meaning just go for it without a thought. At this point on Friday night, I was invincible and feeling good. The world was my oyster. I was going to see family, and that was it. I jumped in my car, thinking I was okay, and I stopped by the liquor store one more time. My whiskey was calling me, and so was my music along with this beautiful Friday night. And now I am off.

I am not conscious. Laying in a bed, feeling stiff as hell with one eye open, my mouth completely shut and there is nothing but black shadows. I am all in my head talking to GOD or for some-one to hear I am done. I cannot do this anymore; I am ready to **die**. Instantly after this request, I am woken up yet with a full understanding of where I am although I knew who was in front of me. There are three cousins from Clinton, Maryland. I acknowledge them, but in the back of my mind, I am thinking, what happened, and how in the hell did I get here? Oh, by the way, I am in a hospital bed in a room with devices all around me and in me.

This post-concussion syndrome is a **beast**. I do remember somewhat about the hospital, con-sidering I was in there for a total of 10 days, half the time in ICU and the other half up on the sixth floor in a regular hospital room. This must be a damn nightmare. I am learning basic life skills all over again. My girl, my mother, and my aunt are all looking at me with sympathy, but I am feeling embarrassed and full of shame. I need help, and how am I going to get it? I cannot even think about this accident anymore. Am I the only one hurt from this all?

CHAPTER 3

EXAMINING

Alarm is set at 6 a.m. Okay, I am up. What does this day have for me? I am feeling so-so, I am not going to lie; I'm really not making any sense about what is going on. I wash up and head to breakfast. The day has started, and I am up before my room-mate, still in structure mode and seeing what this place has to offer and check-ing my feelings at the gate. The last time I felt like this was in prison. So many personalities, and I can see we all are battling something inside. Can I do this and deal? GOD knows what I need and how to break me down. At this point right now, my mouth will not speak. It's just silence inside like, *be quiet and just listen.* Examine what is around and let the feelings of others mentor to you. There is nothing wrong with listening and being open. I can say that not thinking about the outside has no impact on my thinking of what is around me. I am totally new to this process and the vulnerability of being around people who have the disease of some kind of addiction.

Fighting is what I want to do with this situation. If only these feelings were a punching bag. Who do some of these individuals think they are? You all are dealing with the same thing I am. Not going to fake the feeling, but I am not into this right now. Can I do this?

I am around individuals I do not know the majority of the day to talk about how I am feeling and why I did some of the things I did in the past and cur-rent future. I know people come into your life for a reason and a season, but, really, leave me alone. I got a lot I am dealing with. Since my birthday weekend of July 31, 2019, until now things in my life have been crazy. So much is going on in my life, plus dealing with my current and past decisions. I heard to give it time. The fact is that I am impatient and a very emotional person who can and does act out if it makes me very uncomfortable.

CHAPTER 4

BEING EXPOSED

I am starting off with one of my peers going home today. I surely am happy inside for him, but seriously, the day (a.m.) is not starting off on a positive note. For some reason, I am not in the mood for all this day, but I show up and keep it silent. As we are giving our goodbyes, (individually and collectively), there is a range of topics included in the goodbye. What really sticks with me with our goodbyes is the joy, gratitude, struggles and goals. Everyone, I feel, poured their hearts into it, and I just want to say, "Be quiet." Damn, does everyone in here have an answer, including the staff too? Oh, well, let us see how this goes.

She is asking a lot of me already as we start. Maybe it is my response to her question. Her: "How is your day is going?" Me: "I am just not here today, and I am not feeling this." She is like, "Tell me about it." Me: I am going through a lot mentally, physically, and emotionally. The counselor's response to me: "You are one person who has gone through a lot in your life, and you have only been in this inpatient program for just a couple of days. It is alright not to expose yourself and let strangers in but give yourself some time. Adjust, and yes, you have endured a lot. But that is why you are here, to take steps in finding your way and finding yourself again, but most of all, 'coping.'"

What I am learning in this program, process and or system is it is going to put you in a vulnerable state. Now, I am just speaking for me. I do not like it. Others want an ear. I have always been that ear to others, but what she was saying was to be that person who let it go and not keep it bottled up like a pipe with too much pressure. You know what happens when too much pressure fills the pot on the stove or overflows that cup or too much air in a balloon, it busts.

I am somewhat relieved after talking to her, and yet it is still early in the day, there is still more interaction with my peers and others to go. Can I do this? I am telling you, for every time I think about this, it has me stuck. Honestly, if I could only stop time and just yell out loud, "Can I do this?" Is that too much to ask?

So, I ran into my good friend as I like to think. This older woman I met in here and connected with in so many ways. I start to share about my session with the mental health doctor and with other things discussed. It is crazy when you know you have met a good person. You ask yourself, "Where the hell have you been?" On a serious note, we are talking to each other, and then a remarkable coincidence comes out, we both have the same birthday. What are the odds of that? We are laughing about it but happy because we both agreed we have never met anyone with the same birthday. Cool, huh? I feel obligated to let her know I started journaling. She is like, "Yeah, I am surprised my counselor didn't mention that to me." I am like, "Well, this was started by me, something in me just said, 'Start it.'" She asks to read it, and I am like, "Sure." I told her I was even thinking of making this a book for others who have had the same experience as me, or, having this be their first, second, or third inpatient program. She starts reading my book, and as I am watching her reactions, there is seriousness, smiles, and questions. One statement she says is, "You are an upfront person." I am like, "Yeah. Holding back is not my character or personality." She just nods her head and keeps reading. Then there is a pause, and out of nowhere, she is like, "Now I see why you did not talk this morning." (Exposed.) I am like, "Huh. What do you mean?"

She indicates that what I wrote earlier in the chapter was why I did not speak. I had to think on this because, honestly, I am just journaling and hitting this paper here, letting it all out. I'm tired of keeping these feelings in. I want to see others happy and make people happy. Darn, I even want others to like me too, but nowa-days, everyone is so damn sensitive, and you cannot even be real with people (some).

CHAPTER 5

A SINGLE STEP

Early morning rising, and my roommate is leaving. I did not really build a real connection with him, but he is a humble and focused guy, I can tell, when he puts his mind to something. I start with a routine every morning making my smoothies. Some people are up playing spades and cards, and so on. This one guy, I cannot remember his name, we just did not and still do not connect, but we say good morning to each other. I guess it was one of those things where we are just taking a single step toward human interactions and connection. I do not even know him from Adam and Eve, and my instinct is to go to him and ask, "What's the deal," meaning, why are you so uptight with me? But the other side of me is like, "Oh, well, I will not see you anymore in a couple of weeks." Funny how the new reading material from my daily devotion tells me to throw off everything that hinders me and the transgressions that so easily entangle me, the reaction and actions of others that just do me a certain way. I hold on to it like it killed someone in my family. I guess another part of my therapy here is letting things go and not letting it worry me so much. Still more on this day to come. Stay tuned...

Two guys are leaving this morning, and part of my new daily devotion had me share this with one of them this morning. "Choose friends who are also committed to the race." Wrong friends will have values and activities that may deter you from the course. Much of your own weight may result from the crowd you run with. Make wise choices. It was awkward at one point, but I barely knew him. And who am I to share with someone I barely know, I just got here. But the GOD of my understanding had me share with this guy what I had read earlier. It was just like I read this guy's mind. He tells me with tears in his eyes, face red as a tomato, and cheeks about swollen that he is going to call his dealer friend, tell him he is out, and he is doing good and blah, blah, blah. I am like, "No, you said you wanted to continue to have a personal relationship with GOD. Well, here you are, and he is literally speaking to you." The guy that was leaving just comes up closer and hugs me tightly and says, "Thank you so much." I tell him to call or go to a NA or AA meeting. "Use the contacts you have established since being here." Ironic, isn't it—how we can ask for help, and when we get that message or sign, it is right there in front of us, and it is so quick to be answered, not when we want it, but right on time.

CHAPTER 6

FILLING IN

So, it is the weekend and hopefully, this program is a little more laid back. I am still sore as hell from the workout on Friday but it feels good to be back in the gym since my car accident. I will fill you guys and gals in on that topic. My story is messed up, but I am still here. Filling in, I guess, and being honest with you all about being in this inpatient program, it has had it's ups and downs. Dealing with my personal drama, issues, dilemmas, struggles, and so on, I have been on a damn emotional roller coaster. Should I leave and just say, "The heck with it?" I am not up for other people's attitudes toward me; I do not know you and do not know why you are acting this way toward me. I could go on and on, but I guess I am just venting. The counselors seem to be good people and want the best. I would have to say that most of them have had addiction issues too, but that does not help the matter. So, they feel where I am coming from.

This Saturday morning does take a lot out of me, though, talking about my father and his way of leaving me the way he did; committing suicide, like, you inconsiderate ass person, you left me. I shared this morning on the topic of "Being Willing." Basically, I am "filling in," like the name of this chapter, considering I am in here like everyone else and I need to or should be willing to share and be open. If I am tired of being depressed, mad, sad, anxious, and helpless, then I should share where I am at or at least what is on my mind because there is no wrong or right feeling. You are feeling what you are feeling because it is affecting your life in a negative way. Yes, a burden is lifted. It still hurts and sucks, but at least I let it out.

We got to go on an outing, which was not bad at all. Yes, I am hanging out with total strangers I do not know, but we had a great time. Mini golf in the neon setting was fun, and some Italian food to cap it off hit the spot. Not bad at all, and still more of the day to finish. I am getting there, opening up to the program and people. There is a reason I am here. I am on my knees everyday asking for revelation. Now, I am allowing some good and bad energy to be exposed. I guess I just gotta let it fill in so I can learn how to deal with it.

The weekend really had calmed my nerves, but still, that little pinched nerve gave me a headache all weekend. I am calm as I can be but still nervous about my family visit this weekend. Church is uplifting, the smiles and welcomes are so inviting for us from the inpatient facility. Family day continues with Sunday, and everyone is all smiles and no negative energy. My girlfriend comes by and acts like she had never seen me before, which makes the departing much more painful. I must admit that this experience is becoming less stressful with each waking moment. Certainly, the one on ones have been helpful.

I have never been active in AA meetings or NA meetings, which have had different impacts on me. I am not going to lie; a lot of times, it is hard to relate to some of the people's experiences but hear-ing their trials and tribulations has me thinking of some of my actions and my less thoughtful situa-tions of my actions that have affected family and friends.

As a growing process in this journey, one of the key things I have learned or come to learn is "What is freedom truly?" The basic test of freedom is not in what we are free to do but rather in what we are free not to do! Today, we are free not to drink or do drugs. For me, this really breaks down the word and action of acting my freedom out. This is a serious disease that I/we struggle with. For those coming into an impatient recovery treatment center for the first time or multiple times, please, I am not a specialist at this after six days, coming to terms with and accepting where I am and what I have become. It somewhat makes me understand why and what I have been struggling with. Taking it one day at a time has really been helping me. I have come to this lesson

that I cannot worry about what is outside, but I pray to the GOD of my understanding to handle all my affairs pertaining to the outside of the inpatient's walls. This has really been my ground of foundation and, so far, has gotten me through.

CHAPTER 7

HOLIDAY DAY

It is Christ's birthday today, and it started well. The service last night at church spoke volumes. Two different services were held at a nearby local church in Glen Burnie, Maryland (LightHouse). We attended the second service, and it was still a packed church house. A lot of us (ten) from the house came to hear a message. The other four stayed home, but surely, they were in our thoughts and prayers. A lot of revelation was acknowledged by all ten of us, and that was a blessing. Talk about needing to hear something or get some answers to the questions you have; I have to say my higher power (Jesus Christ) was right on time. The Spirit was in that place last night. No complaints here, just gratitude and a joyful spirit we all left with. I love seeing people smiling and having hope in their hearts. It gives me hope and a peaceful view toward the future and me knowing that I have a choice to not drink or do drugs.

For some reason, I was very restless that night when trying to sleep. I could not get it together and was sweating a little bit too. I know my shoulder was still aching, but I knew it was something else too. Time passed; at first, it was 1:32 a.m. I got up and used the bathroom, then went to sleep. My roommate got up at like a quarter to 5 a.m., and I was like, no way, and okay, carry on. I am going back to sleep.

It feels like I have not written in a while considering these past weekend's festivities, let alone a lot of drama; arguments over the TV, people's personal space being violated, staff (some) not respecting some of the residents (self), some people's attitudes, and understanding that I am in a co-ed facility and there is going to be quarrels every now and then. Attitudes are going to be wishy washy. The difference here and dealing with the outside world is my reaction to not pick up a drink or use drugs. Being eleven days into this inpatient treatment center and in an enclosed facility has taught me a lot about how to cope with pressure, and, my word of choice, drama. Being somewhat under the weather does not help, but stepping out of my comfort zone and using the tools that have been given gives me a different light on any subject. My personal one on ones with my counselor have really helped, bringing forth all the issues that have played my inner emotions like a fiddle. Again, I am not so much caring about the outside but still being real with myself about court, my bills, rent, job, and so on. The only way of overcoming these feelings and emotions is giving it to GOD, my higher power.

Sitting in my vacant room now and writing out my feelings is okay and feels good. Yes, the rest of the house is noisy as heck, but alone time feels so right. We are about to have a packed house, a huge dinner with all our loved ones for a holiday combination of Christmas and New Year's dinner. It will be interesting having us all together. Mixed and happy emotions are everywhere. Here is my care of what others are feeling and thinking. Like my counselor told me, I need to think and take care of myself first at times. "Quality takes time, and you are GOD's Masterpiece" (T.D. Jakes...).

GOD has a strategy in the ugly places of our lives because those are the fields in which he decided to cultivate us (T. D. Jakes). In agreement with this, I now conclude that GOD is cultivating me and overturning the negative character defects in my life.

Carrying our worries, stress, and daily struggles by ourselves shows that we have not fully trusted GOD with our lives. It takes humility, however, to recognize that GOD cares, to admit our need, and to let others in GOD's family help us. Sometimes we think that our struggles are caused by our own sin and foolishness; we think it is not GOD's concern, but when we turn to our higher power in repentance, he will bear the weight of even those harsh struggles. Letting GOD have our anxieties calls for action and passivity. Do not submit to circumstances but to the LORD, who controls circumstances.

CHAPTER 8

SLAYING THE DRAGON

Psalm 30;11–12: "You turned my wailing into dancing; you removed my sackcloth and clothed me with joy, that my heart may sing your praises and not be silent. Lord my GOD. I will praise you forever."

There will be days when I hurt, feel stuck, or do not believe there is much to celebrate. As I am learning in this program of AA and NA, there are sure to be some hard times in my recovery for sure. Starting this process to slay the dragon has been one of those moments of closed-mouth pondering. Each process toward this recovery, or slaying, has been an emotional drain. Talking every day with one of my counselors and mental health therapist drains the feelings out of me, but this day, I somewhat knew it would test my mental strength.

After the gym and coming home to set up for this appointment as a new client, it has me inquisitive. I have seen one of the friends I met in this inpatient program come up from downstairs. She has this "I do not know what happened" look. By the way, her name is Michelle. A bond between us has developed quickly with trust, honesty, and has been supporting enough to know when something is up.

Her story is much like mine; alcohol addiction (the same) was her choice of substance. She has a strong personality and speaks what is on her mind, has two children, is married, and a teacher. She did not need company to enjoy alcohol and stay in her head, for the most part, of all the different situations that appeared in her life. We (other clients) in the house love her energy and realness toward responses to conversations in group settings. Michelle has her struggles, and she talks with me over my same hang-ups. Both our mothers were so identical with their choice of words to us as children growing up. Not smart, not going anywhere, and would tell us both we would not amount to anything. I mean, why say that to your own child?

Thinking about this just makes me angry. And no, I do not want to drink after this, but part of this process is one step closer to complete healing in our lives. So, "Mike" is waiting for me in the acupuncture room as I change clothes. I come into the room scared, nervous, and ready. The room is dim, and the table is set up for observation, but he asks me first what was the first thing about my father that I felt was a positive influence in my life. I told him his willingness to not be a quitter, and my father stressed/valued education very much. Then after that conversation, I feel like I go into dark thoughts when he asks what were the negative

My Father

Influences that came from the relationship with my father. Now, my father was a master chief in the Navy and had served for twenty years in the military. He was very career-driven, loving at times when he was not drinking. But still, I felt like I did not know him, being his oldest son. He and my mother would fight at times, and it would get very physical. As the acupuncture session gets more in-depth, the more I get angry, but I did get angrier with the questions being asked. I am left in the room in the dark to sit and meditate on what has just transpired. I noticed my hand start to fold into a fist, and my attitude quickly changed. Then Mike, the acupuncture specialist, walks in, and we close out the session on a good note.

The treatment center I am in is getting us ready for an outside AA/NA meeting. There is no time to really process and digest what I am experiencing. "Slaying the dragon" would be useful explains Mike, but consider it cleansing, which I do. My father was 5'10" with a short-haired faded haircut style, brown eyes, and 205 lb. Quite a quiet person for the most part from what I had seen and who did not say much at first, but when a subject was brought up within his interest, he would respond with passion. As I could see, he did not really bond with my mother's brothers a lot because of his actions to-ward our immediate family and especially my mother. When it came to my mother, it ended up in verbal and physical abuse. He took pride and seriousness in his military career, an accountable militaria to his appointed squadron. I just wish he were attentive to his family as well. My father and my sister were very tight, and I feel they were like best friends, something I wish he and I were. I guess I was not transparent with wanting more in our father-and-son relationship. My brother was incredibly young before my father's death, and there was not a lot of bonding. I did not know too much about my father's upbringing very well or his and his father's relationship. A lot of shade was throughout my dad's side of the family, but I did know they drank alcohol a lot when visiting. I guess that was their way of communicating effectively or felt that was needed to communicate.

CHAPTER 9

SMALL CHANGES/ HITTING ROCK BOTTOM

Ephesians 4:22–24; Matthew 11:28

Prayer:

Father, I want peace of mind. I have been captive to my painful, troubling, disobedient thoughts for far too long. As I surrender to you, surround myself with good people and flood my mind with your Word. I pray that you will bring me the gift of peace.

Change still isn't easy for me. What I am learning is that making small changes makes it much easier to make big changes when needed. This experience brought me a friend, Brad, whom I met in here. It started out difficult for him but its helped him (and myself) get rid of negative thoughts and mindsets. We as individuals can have some similar ways of thinking but different life experiences which shows in how we internalize life and cope with our internal feelings.

Brad is a very humble person. Coming from a successful family background, he is the youngest of a sibling brother and has a precious little girl. An introvert, I feel, in a new setting, but he can easily blend in once he's in a comfortable space for himself. He engages in just about any subject when he feels comfortable discussing. Brad is not new to this inpatient program process, as he indicated to me. As time is going on, he is showing signs of wellness. When he first got there, he stopped shaving the left side of his face in the morning, and then started to do both sides. I told him, "Bro, that is awesome." To get something you never had, you must do something you have never done before.

We hit rock bottom when we finally get tired of being beat up by ourselves and others. Brad and I totally relate to each other on this level. When lives became completely unmanageable, from isolation, substance abuse, and near death experiences, we have an awakening. Peace of mind is what we want like everyone else, which we are having trouble finding. Digging our holes deeper by flooding our thoughts with the bad thinking that has gotten us where we are now. Can I do this? Whether it's another treatment program, starting a new inpatient intensive program, or just being open to letting a stranger into my thoughts. These are some of the questions that we as clients have. Peace of mind is attainable, but it requires a new lifestyle, new habits, new behaviors, and relationships that are strong and upright. I know with GOD's help I can find my way, but nothing less than complete commitment will get me there. I am noticing Brad is starting to know who GOD is and developing that intimate relationship. I have shared my faith with him about GOD, not getting too much into the religious part of it but explaining to him the intimate relationship he could continue to strengthen by a continuous connection with his higher power. Everyone comes into your life for a reason and a season. This journey is doing more than enough to have me believe this statement. At this point of complete surrendering, how do we find rest?

CHAPTER 10

THE VISIT

Father, what a gift I have found in forgiving and receiving forgiveness. Thank you for your goodness to me. In Jesus's name, amen

It is an inquisitive day on Sunday, our family visiting day, but I am calm when attending church. I do not know what to expect with my visit with Momma Dukes. That word "Momma Dukes" is an African-American colloquialism. Not letting my emotions get the best of me is my goal for that day. Seeing some old clients from the treatment center at church this morning is good. They are sober and seem to be in good spirits, at peace, and smiling. It gives me hope on my release date and the days to come after that. The sermon is focused on the word *supreme*, which refers to putting GOD first in all you do. Let him be first in your life, letting forgiveness rest in your heart, letting go of the past, and looking forward to which is ahead. It is ironic at times for me when I start my day with him. That early morning meditation can have you rooted but grounded, using GOD's words and instructions on how to live, to help you get through. Receiving forgiveness for my past acts when in old alcoholic ways, forgiving others that may have judged me when I was not me, and knowing that the spirit that was in me was not me at all at times. So, in all, I am growing, but in a sense, I am letting my higher power have his way with me.

Right before the visit, I am very anxious. I am pacing back and forth, thinking about how this family session is going to go. Will I be able to maintain my emotions, whether sad or happy? To be completely free from my resentments, anger, fears, shame, and guilt, I need to give and accept forgiveness in all areas of my life. My mother coming plays a big role in my receiving and giving forgiveness. I am not sure if she will accept and understand my state of mind and my reasons for drinking alcohol. Walking toward the treatment center, I am having all these thoughts. My heart is pounding, and mouth is very dry from my anxiety toward meeting with her. The last time we talked was not so pleasant, it was same day I came to the treatment center. What a heck of a way to start this new journey!

My mother is a very hard-working woman and very opinionated. She came from a family of six children. Worked extremely hard as she was growing up, with a strong personality and speaking what was on her mind, she stood up for battle whenever she felt her sister or brother was being picked on. Her father was a factory worker and drank a lot of alcohol, and her mother was a home nurse for the elderly. My mother took care of all three of us, my sister, brother, and myself. She always tried to make sure we had all we needed plus more. While my father was on deployment, she was a super mom, taking care of everything in the household.

Seeing her come in the front door is a happy moment, and I hug her tightly and do not want to let her go. She is happy to see me too. My counselor escorts my mother, girlfriend, and me downstairs to our family meeting location, which is in the yoga room. We all sat and smiled at each other as my counselor initiated the meeting. She gave an introduction of my progress here, what we are working on, and where I am in my treatment. I was sitting there pondering where to start and what to say during their visit. My counselor asks me to begin talking about my current state of mind and where I am, and I begin. Not, even five minutes into my conversation, I am crying simultaneously, discussing why I drank alcohol, my father, and how my mother made me feel over the years. I cannot even look her in the eyes. That is when my counselor interferes and says that I am dealing with depression and had been this way for a long time. While this is happening, I am just gathering my thoughts and looking at my girlfriend as her eyes are watering up too. I can see my mother is in shock trying to process this and choking up as well. My mother begins to say she did not know this about me but was also under the impression that my father's death did play a part in my mood swings and sadness. So, I know she figured something was there but did not know the severity of how this really affected me. As a family, we mourned over my father's death but never checked in with each over the loss. I am referring to my immediate family: my brother, sister, mother, and myself. Quickly, my counselor changes the subject as we go into other topics because she knows that I am hurting, and it is hurting my mother. So, to be continued at the next family session. Our visit is limited, and we want to talk about other things like my discharge plan and a plan of action moving forward to help me stay sober. This visit is needed for sure for both parties, my mother and myself. We can leave the family session on a good note, and I am able to continue to show my mouther around this huge house we call the treatment cen-ter. She meets with some of my peers. It is soothing, but I need for her to see and experience this with me. We sit around talking and catching up, my mother, my girlfriend, and I, over some delicious meatballs. Never have I eaten the same thing twice while being at this place. It seems like old times, just talking and catching up, but still a lot of open wounds that need to be addressed. I just enjoy the moment. Oh, how a visit can bring in and give out forgiveness.

She sits up, right shoulders pinned back, hands crossed and, in her lap, straight face, and listening to the information given to her. There is concern in her voice and immediately I can tell she is already trying to figure out a solution to my problem. Being a parent and seeing your child struggle with something that is causing harm to him or her is a burden you carry. My mother has enough stress and worries. I surely do not want to add fuel to the conversation, which I know I am already too emotional to carry on with and can't take any more emotional stress. Seeing and hearing her reply is a relief and comforting. My girlfriend knows a lot about my family and father's death. Her presence sets more comfort to "The Visit." She is very silent with her head nodding, just partaking in the family meeting. I have to say she has been more than a backbone for me in this process, and for her to sit in and listen to all my family has been through and still be here is a blessing. She has her past and things she has had to overcome from her family as well. Salute to her loyalty as a person, girlfriend, and friend. It feels good to have support from someone who loves you and is still getting to know you as a person. She does not count flaws, as many as we all have as human beings, but her just being here lets me know in action, "I got your back," means a lot. Some of us have this kind of support, and some of us do not. It is not to say I am better than the ones who do not have it. We all have that loved one who is praying for us. We just do not realize until a certain situation in our lives happens, which causes us to wake up. It is crazy how blind to life we get when are caught up in our addiction. I am starting to learn in this recovery process to pay attention to those seemingly small nudges, which often come through other people. They help keep me grounded and moving in the right direction. My prayer: "Most gracious and loving Father, thank you for leading me gently through my life, refocusing me to fulfill your purpose. In Jesus's name, amen."

CHAPTER 11

You Got to Dance with the One who Brought You Here

Prayer:

Father, thank you for the care and tools you have given
me to live a successful life. I want to be all you created
me to be. In Jesus's precious name, amen.

Who would have ever known that, along with depression, my
father's death, anxiety, and not being where I want to be suc-
cessfully in my life to this point, were all reflections of my excessive
drinking? The trouble is, on our own, we lack the resources and understanding we need to avoid disasters. Most of us find that out the hard way.
Or we try to live our lives according to society's norms and expectations.

I know my father wanted the best for his children, especially when
it came to education. Yes, he was a hard act to follow expectation-wise,
but there definitely were exciting moments with him. When my mother
left, it was just my father and me. He was shocked at the end results of
his actions from alcohol that had lasted for years, and my mother had
enough of it. I was not surprised at her wanting to leave. This goes back
to that nineties' song, "When a Woman Is Fed Up." When she was done,
she showed it. I just knew in my heart that this move would bring me

and my father closer. The whole point of coming to this inpatient facility is to "dance with the problem" that brought me here, and believe me, I have danced, cried, built anger, and questioned these emotions.

Now, there were special moments with my father that I will never forget, especially when I would come home from school (high school). He would open the windows in all the living and dining rooms, and he would play jazz music (like Najee) that would vibrate through the house as I would be doing my homework. His experience in the kitchen as he prepared dinner was like no other. This, to me, was father and son time, and I would call him to the table when I needed help. He never hesitated with helping me. For some reason, at a young age, I liked and respected this. He even got me a job at a local limousine shop detailing the vehicles. This was his part-time gig next to being in the military. I figured he was teaching me responsibility as well. I felt that this was necessary to teach me how to be a young man. Nothing was better than that. My father was not perfect, but what I had learned was that he was doing the best he could at his own strength and understanding. Holding on to the good and bad memories had their benefits. Being here in inpatient was helping me balance the memories and cope with why and how this happened.

CHAPTER 12

MY TURN

If we do not pay attention, we are apt to fall backward into old hurts, hang-ups, and habits.

Tuesday night is our night for inside meetings. We all gathered in the conference room, waiting for our speaker. Everyone is accounted for and anticipating what message and guest speaker we will have. As I sit back in my chair, I see one of the PAs (program assistant) come into the conference room and ask me to share my story since I am the up-and-coming next client to go home. My heart drops, and it starts beating rapidly. Talk about weakness; I know my face shows possible defeat. And me being human, you can see I do not want others seeing my weakness and frowning upon me. As I am getting up, a friend from the program, Megan, volunteers to assist me in facilitating the group. She gets everyone's attention and totally takes control in getting everyone on one accord. I am not going to lie, I am vulnerable to the process, but I want and need to be sober. As I start out with my story, I am so nervous I am stumbling over my words. Starting from the beginning of my life is easy, but as I continue into the second half, my memory is going in and out. You could've dropped a pen on the carpet of the conference room we are in and hear it. Relinquishing control of my story starts to somewhat get easy. The way I am thinking while sharing is, "To get something you never had, you have to do something you had never done before," Everyone in the room is receptive to my story and respectful. I appreciate that and am incredibly grateful. Who would ever have known that surrendering our story could bring healing to our souls? Sharing my pain was not something I was good at when sober. The only time I could really let go and share my true feelings was when I was drunk. I never knew that expressing your true feelings about something so hurtful could be so relieving. As I get to the end of the story, so many hands are raised up for responses and comments. I never knew that sharing was the answer to showing sympathy and care. Everyone received the message and could relate. Again, you would never realize that to get something you never had, you have to do something you had never done before. Kudos to this inpatient treatment. Who would have ever known this step into my new sober living would lift the yoke from around my neck?

The more I take in, the comments, concerns, and responses, the more relief overtakes me. Sooner or later, I learn that true freedom comes when I open myself to the hard-learned wisdom that others provide. Some of the clients in the room cannot believe the situations I endured growing up as a child. They respect the fact that I would share my story. One of my best friends, Joe, asks me to share some of this book with the group. I freeze and start to clench my composition book with fear for some reason. I have not really shared my work with the rest of the clients here, but the after-effect is rewarding. Continued comments of how I endured my past is brought up. "Jamel, from Steve, 'I would have never guessed that about you and how you are still here.'" Encouraging individuals is amazing. To be honest, my journey to this point has made me the person I am today. I have a self-made portrait for the new 2020-year vision board by my bed with a picture of my children up next to it. In the middle of my vision board is a quote by Asha Tyson. It says, "Your journey has molded you for the greater good. This is exactly what it needed to be. Do not think you have lost time. It took each situation you have encountered to bring you the now. And now is right on TIME." How true is this? My mistakes, fears, and doubts are my path to wisdom. The most important things I'm learning today are peace, personal accomplishments, celebration of life, love, respect, self-respect, and to understand and be understood. Most of all my higher power, which is GOD, is who I need conscious contact with on a daily.

CHAPTER 13

EVERYTHING HAPPENS FOR A REASON/AWAKEN

Prayer:

My words cannot express your greatness. Things always
go better when I surrender.

This day is starting exceedingly early (6 a.m.). A day passes till I
must handle my personal affairs and court issues in another state.
My objective starts out with only two things to accomplish on my to-do
list. This Thursday should not be that bad. What I am learning here and
starting to apply to my life daily is the Serenity Prayer: "GOD grant me
the serenity to accept the things I cannot change, courage to change the
things I can, and the wisdom to know the difference," from the Just for
Today! There is so much truth in this quote. My girlfriend is here right
on time and greets me with a smile and a hug. I have to say it feels nice
to be missed. Some of my roommates/clients are already up and ready
to get this day going. It is still dark outside and a little chilly, but I am
grateful to smell the morning dew. And we are off.

Not even fifteen to twenty minutes into the drive, my girlfriend
asks me about my lease that expires four months down the road of the
new year. I am in my head like, *Really? Right Now?! Can I just smell
the morning dew first for a little bit before we get into deep serious*

conversations about life and our future together? My mind at this point is really on all that I must handle on this day, which is stress within its own self. Life is waiting for me to come out from this inpatient program. I feel like it is already doing push-ups and building itself up, and it is going to hit me all at once, which it already has. But I am remaining calm, and my first stop is my apartment. I want to check on things before I go where I need to go. Talk about feeling like a stranger in my own home. Honestly, it feels weird and uncomfortable; being totally disconnected from the world takes on a whole new meaning. I feel like the little kid in me wants to say "Take me back home to the inpatient program facility. In my heart, I know I have to show up with internal strength and ask GOD to help me get through this day. We still have another hour and a half to get to our first destination, which I am nervous about. I could possibly go to jail this day because of a violation of the bond I was out on. The **show** must continue.

What freedom it brings to know that when we are powerless, we have an ally to help us through the hard times. Today, for me, is one of those hard days. So, as we are approaching our destination, my heart is rapidly beating, hands trembling, mouth parched, and exhaustion kicking in. All these feelings and emotions happen seconds upon arriving. We walk into the establishment, and I pick up the commercial-like house phone in the brick police precinct. The operator asks me what my visit is about, and I explain. She tells me to sit a minute, and someone will assist me momentarily. You would think I am about to see the president the way I am acting, but I remain calm. So much activity is going on at this facility. I do not mention where I am because of how I feel; I do not say anything about where I am at the time. I am getting my fingerprints done. Do not ask the state where I am having all this done; they do things differently. I will leave it like that.

As we are patiently waiting, I decide to make some phone calls and get my bills paid for and up to date. So, I step outside to get it taken care of, not really knowing what is going on inside. I decide to step back in because it is cold outside, and my girlfriend mentions something to me. I cannot really hear her, and I ask her to mention to me again what it is she is trying to say. Her reply is, "The officer who wrote you the charges was here at the facility. My mouth drops and eyes get bigger, you would think I saw a ghost, and my nerves are trembling in my hands. In my head, I am like, *this is it*. I just know I am going to jail. Talk about a coincidence. Out of all these days and timing, he has to be there at the same time and place I am. At this point, I am **awake**; everything happens for a reason. Again, let us get this show on.

So, he comes out and says, "Mr. Freeman are you ready?" I tell him, "Yes, I am." He has a straight stern look on his face, so I cannot really tell his mood at the present time. His request before we go anywhere, is to run a scanner detector over my person to make sure I do not have any weapons or contraband because we are in a police precinct. There can be no hard metal objects or harmful devices on any person coming to get fingerprinted. I assume the position, and he scans me up and down. We proceed to walk down the hall, which isn't new to me, the smell of old wall brick paint and metal toilets in a police station. We walk into the fingerprinting room. He asks me to take a seat while he sets up the computer to start the process. I am just stuck at this point and make no movement, not even a twitch, feeling like a teenager about to see the principal in middle school. He turns to me and says, "How are you?" I tell him I am doing okay, health-wise. It is a slow process but making progress. He says, "You look like you are healing pretty well and look totally different from what you looked like after the car accident in the back of the ambulance." I tell him, "I am healing pretty well and getting back to normal, slowly but surely." He exclaims, "I did not think you were going to make it. You were just lying there, and the paramedics were just pumping you, trying to get you to breathe and help you to not choke on your own blood. There was blood everywhere." I just sit there with my mouth completely dropped to the ground with nothing to say. He says, "I have seen a lot of accidents, and not saying yours was not bad, but I've seen worst. But you, Mr. Freeman, are a lucky man." I just put my head down, and I say, "You are right, sir." I start to explain to him what I am doing while in body recovery. I tell him I am in an inpatient facility and addressing the issues of my causes to why I drink alcohol, to feel and not feel emotions. I tell him about my father and how he committed suicide. I explain to the police officer that my father was a master chief in the Navy and served twenty years in active service. The officer then indicates that he was in the military too, and he tells me he was in combat infantry. He does say to me that he is apologetic about what happened to my father and gives his regards. He then calls me up to start the fingerprinting process. So, we just go back and forth with good conversation pertaining to military life, and so on. Then he asks me to go to the sink after we are done to wash my hands off. As I am doing this, he comes and stands next to me holding some paper towels. After I am done washing, he hands me the paper towels. A somewhat awkward moment, but I am just living in the moment as I dry my hands off. I turn to him and apologize for my actions, which had caused him to have to deal with my poor decisions that evening/ morning, indicating to him also that my life had become unmanageable, and I am serious about seeking help. As I am saying this, I extend my hand out to shake his. With no hesitation, he extends his too. He gives me a look as if he feels what I am feeling, which is compassion and sympathy. I know these officers deal with traumatic situations every day, but I want him to know I have respect for him. I can tell he is surprised and relieved. After our sympathetic moment is over, he asks me to follow him back to the front. I go through the door and just plump myself down in the chair like I am devastated. So many emotions run through me. My girl asks what happened. Oh, by the way, the officer did mention for me to not leave for a few minutes. I have to wait to make sure my fingerprints are accepted and cleared. I tell my girlfriend about the unforgettable experience I have had with the officer. She just looks at me with proud eyes and says that officer was a nice man and will not forget this experience he just had with me. Seconds later, the officer comes out and tells me I am free to go. He also says to take care of myself and continue to seek treatment, that we may see each other again. Talk about an everything-happens-for-a-reason moment. Divine timing has just brought on a new meaning. So, we leave, and I leave with peace, amends, and a quiet spirit. Still, we have more places to go.

So, next is the local probation office I have to check into. Again, nerves jumping, I tell myself I will never go through this again. So, we go into the establishment. I tell the clerk at the front desk my name, and she says to have a seat. I wait patiently for my temporary probation officer to come get me. As I am waiting, I see all these other people getting occupied by other probation officers going into the back or clients leaving. My probation officer finally shows up, and from what I can tell, she is cool, calm, and collected, not your typical probation officer. Some do have that look on them like, *do not mess with me*. Thank GOD mine is chill. So, we proceed to the back to her office. She asks me to take a seat, and I do. She starts to ask about things from my past to present, to give my word and what I am up to now. I basically just tell her the same as what I told the officer of what I am doing now and my intentions after my inpatient treatment is over. This meeting goes very quickly, I must say, and again, nervous as I was there because I know I violated my bond and did not know if there was a warrant out for me or not. Thus far I am clear.

So, the two major assignments I had to have done by this day are accomplished, but then there are still other phone calls and errands that come up that I have to attend to. I just know deep down, before I had to leave, this will be a busy day for tasks. Life shows me something else; I have to put some of the steps, traditions, and learned skills to work in this situation: one day at a time, living in the now, accepting some things for what they were, and changing the things that I could. Trusting in GOD at this point is all I have. This day becomes very exhausting despite getting something to eat to rejuvenate me. My actions are emotionless. I feel numb to the day. On my way back to the treatment center, I have nothing to talk about. I am just so in my head, but I also honestly can say I do not want to drink. And as I am getting dropped off and saying goodbye till Sunday (family visiting day), I walk back up to the inpatient treatment center, shouting in my head, "I WON!"

CHAPTER 14

AM I SAVED?

It is an early morning wake-up for me. I am almost packed up, and my roommate, Uncle, is still asleep. I do not know if I am more excited about breakfast, the leaving ceremony, just to be home, or nervous about what is ahead. You know when you get those tight muscles in your stomach when something is about to unravel? Well, here goes nothing.

Walking into the kitchen, everyone is somewhat up. I am greeted by one of the morning's PAs (program assistants) and the morning chef. Yes, if I did not mention, we have our own chef. I have been here thirty-eight days and have never eaten the same thing twice. Impressive, right?! Chef K, which is her name, said, "I made this particular breakfast for you since this is your last morning with us"; fluffy waffles, scrambled eggs, sausage, and some cold-ass orange juice. You know what I am thinking? Drenching my waffles in syrup.

The morning proceeds to our 9 a.m. duty meeting and ceremony of me going home. Of course, I am front and center, a little nervous and wondering what others will say as they pass around a coin medallion customized by one of my favorite one-on-one counselors. Sorry, I cannot reveal her name. Another PA is at the front with me and starts off our first summarization conclusions, strength, and hope to give me before leaving. While she is talking, she is passing around my picture from the rehabilitation center first day. The farewell comments are deep, overwhelming, encouraging, and inspiring. I notice myself struggling to swallow and take these messages all in. I am looking outside as the sun is bright and the day is waiting for me, and I ask myself this question in my head, *Am I saved, and am I ready?* Can I do this? My medallion, by the way, is engraved with the Serenity Prayer, "GOD, grant me the serenity to accept the thing I cannot change, courage to change the thing that I can, and the wisdom to know the difference just for today." We all come together at the end to huddle in prayer and close out with our right foot extending out because our left foot left us on the wrong path, the right foot stepping into the right direction. Hugs, handshakes, and teary eyes are exchanged. "Not goodbye but see you later" is what is said.

So, as I am waiting on my ride, looking out at the front door with all my bags packed, I am thinking of all I have learned, unlearned, and experienced while at this rehabilitation unit for my first time. Willing to go through the process is life-changing and scary at the same time. The next level is not knowing what is on the outside waiting for me; work, bills, court dates, family, and health.

The first stop is a sober house living quarters I am supposed to go to, but after my initial visit, it does not go well. My spirit does not settle well, and something deep down tells me no. I am familiar with the living arrangements like this because after incarceration, that's where I went to start on a new path of sober living. Here it was, another recap of a place and situation I used to be in. I thank one of the guys for the opportunity, but I let them know I am going home. I knew deep down I am going to have to buckle down tighter, dig deeper, and surrender more because I have noticed my default to shut down and say, "This is too much; I can do this on my own" when time tells me I cannot, ultimately letting me know to do this one day at a time.

Time has elapsed since being home. Meeting after meeting, IOP three times a week, soon to start a new job, and so many events have happened to me. While in recovery, a pandemic has occurred. Even when I find myself in situations of my own choosing, they become circumstances I was not quite ready for. Attending school now is something new for me, meaning attending online college has taken on a new focus for Jamel. More to come and elaborate on later, but one thing that has helped me is that I have written to my addiction: a poem.

CHAPTER 15

"I MATTER"

Days, weeks, and months have gone by. I am feeling this sober thing. They say, "To get something you never had, you have to do something you've never done before." Truly, staying sober is something in the past I could not do. I was forced, with incarceration as the influencer, to help not drink. Now the tables have turned. It is on me to stay sober. This has truly been a blessing, with the help of AA and NA meetings, IOP, one-on-one counseling, my sponsors, and most of all, my higher power.

When we are in the weeds of things, we have two choices; we could panic or get to work. Panicking is easy, but all it does is waste time and energy, both of which are in short supply. What would be even worse is if I end up right back where I started. Focusing on work, school, relationships, court, family, and getting to work for me is a much better option.

This proves that I am learning in a step-by-step process. My biggest opposition/challenge is one which could send me away for a long time, considering my past youth record and bad decision making. All I have done is not for the satisfaction for the courts but, it is done for myself. Many of us are in the weeds when it comes to our lives and recovery. It seems like I am running as fast as I can and getting nowhere. Not knowing my outcome and just going off pure faith in my higher power is what I have decided to go with and rely on. I found myself in this situation, having to take it one step at a time: every minute, every hour, every day, every week, every month; a step. I will make it if I keep my head up and refuse to panic. My mindset is that "I matter" and one of the hardest things is learning that I am worthy of "recovery."

Funny how all this has played out. I get to keep my new-found job, which I love. I wake up asking GOD to use me and prepare me. The new day is already measured for me, and all I have to do is ask my higher power to help me put things in order. Help me not to panic and show me each new day what I need to do first, and the rest will fall into place. Has this been an emotional roller coaster? Hell, yes! But so far, it has been worth it. The individuals I have met along the way and the lessons I am learning in the process shows me that this is not a drag race; it is progress before perfection.

Noticing my triggers and where my aggravations are coming from, not being all in my head and alone, are so important. They say an idle mind is the devil's workshop. This is so true. He preys on the vulnerable and lonely. I have helped a lot of people since my little bit of time being home and in doing so, have helped myself. This has kept me sober for these seven months.

Authoring this book has been another outlet for me, putting my inner thoughts on paper. It sounds funny when you are talking about it, but the truth is, knowing I am in a world with other individuals who have, somewhat, the same mind-set and go through the same thing I do makes me feel less self-conscious of myself and less like an outcast. Turning up the level on my end for the recovering process has really worked as the enemy/drink has turned up the outside pressures in life.

Again, "I matter," and I am noticing that I can help the next person and myself. A scripture I have found that has been a constant reminder to me in my recovery and readings is:

2 Corinthians 4:8–9

"We are hard pressed on every side by troubles, but we are not crushed; perplexed, but not driven to despair; we are hunted down, but not abandoned; We get struck down, but not destroyed."

Amen to this. Peace and blessings to my fellow sisters and brothers in recovery.

Join us to celebrate the life of
Brad Michael Greenberg
*Brad was a wonderful person
who will be greatly missed.*

When: 7/24/2021, 6-9pm
Where: Foundations Recovery Center
1825 Woodlawn Drive Baltimore, MD 21207

R.I.H
You are Missed Bro.

HALLER

MICHAEL KEITH HALLER

Michael Keith Haller, 24, of Rockville, MD, passed away at his home on July 25, 2020. Michael lived a very full life that was all too short. He was in the process of completing his college education and was working as a Senior Fellow at Ideagen, researching companies that embrace the 17 sustainable goals established by the United Nations.

Michael loved his family, his church, and spending time outdoors. He was passionate about cars, cooking, the military and sports including golf, baseball, hockey, and snowboarding. A devoted fan of the Red Sox, Caps, Nats, and Patriots, he often attended pro games with his friends and parents. Michael had a big heart and a great sense of humor which was evidenced by his frequent and easy, deep laughter. His friends describe Michael as "very caring, always there to listen or to talk, a genuinely kind-hearted human being." Michael served as an altar boy at St. George Greek Orthodox Church, where he also attended services when home in Rockville. At his young age, he had the opportunity to travel extensively, and his favorite trips included Cape Cod, Vermont and Greece - especially Lefkada, Metsovo, and Nymfaio.

Most importantly, Michael loved to spend time with "the cousins," of whom he was the youngest, and looked forward to the family holidays and celebrations that brought them all together. He will be sorely missed by cousins Hollin Elizabeth Pagos of Yarmouth, MA, Katie Pagos Kastoff (Robert) of Mamaroneck, NY, Torrie Pagos Berkey (Adam) of Jersey City, NJ, Dylan Perry (Liza) of Charlestown, MA, Nathan Matticks and Elliott Matticks of Charleston, SC, and Nick Perry of Somerville, MA. Michael was thrilled to learn of the recent births of the next generation of cousins, Sawyer James Kastoff and Rye Charles Perry, shortly before he passed.

Michael is survived by his beloved mother, Stacy Pagos Haller, and by many loving aunts and uncles: Marianne Pagos of Brewster, MA, James Pagos (Barbara) of Eastham, MA, Nancy Perry of Hingham, MA, Annie Matticks (Shawn) of Charleston, SC, Paula Pagos of Boynton Beach, FL, Jeff Lagarias of Ann Arbor, MI, Peter Lagarias (Elaine) of San Rafael, CA, Clark Lagarias (Donna) of Sacramento, CA, and Susan Hoffman of Gaithersburg, MD. Michael's beloved father, G. Keith Haller, predeceased him in 2018.

Due to current COVID-19 restrictions, a private service is being held at St. George Greek Orthodox Church in Bethesda, MD, and private burial in the family plot at Parklawn Memorial Park in Rockville, MD. A memorial service to celebrate Michael's life will be held at a later date.

In lieu of flowers, contributions may be made to the Michael Keith Haller Research Fund at BrightFocus Foundation (www.brightfocus.org)

Please view and sign the online guestbook
www.PumphreyFuneralHome.com

R.I.H.
You are Missed Bro.

Dear Addiction

Here we go again.
To someone at one point, I considered you a friend.
For every time you brought me to a low,
I figured I would write to you and say hello.
Thanks again for reminding me
Of how bad an influence you have been.
Not someone I should ever think about calling a friend.

Your talks at night are a reason for my being independent.

How can I go to the store and even buy you again?

So, as I say goodbye going into the new year,

I will not even miss you

In the up-and-coming New Year.

Printed in the USA
CPSIA information can be obtained
at www.ICGtesting.com
JSHW070835070923
47953JS00008B/24

9 781662 856181